Extracting the Precious From

GaLatians

Bethany House Books
by Donna Partow

Becoming a Vessel God Can Use
Becoming a Vessel God Can Use Prayer Journal
Becoming the Woman I Want to Be
Living in Absolute Freedom
Standing Firm
This Isn't the Life I Signed Up For
This Isn't the Life I Signed Up For AudioBook
This Isn't the Life I Signed Up For Growth Guide
Walking in Total God-Confidence
A Woman's Guide to Personality Types

EXTRACTING THE PRECIOUS
2 Corinthians
Isaiah
Galatians
Nehemiah

EXTRACTING THE PRECIOUS
A BIBLE STUDY FOR WOMEN

Extracting the Precious From

GaLatians

Donna Partow

with Lin Johnson

BETHANYHOUSE
Minneapolis, Minnesota

Published by Bethany House Publishers
11400 Hampshire Avenue South
Bloomington, Minnesota 55438
www.bethanyhouse.com

Bethany House Publishers is a Division of
Baker Book House Company, Grand Rapids, Michigan.

Printed in the United States of America

Library of Congress Cataloging-in-Publication Data

Partow, Donna.
    Extracting the precious from Galatians : a Bible study for women / by Donna Partow with Lin Johnson.
        p.   cm.
    Includes bibliographical references.
    ISBN 0-7642-2698-3 (pbk.)
    1. Bible. N.T. Galatians—Textbooks.   2. Christian women—Religious life—Textbooks.   I. Johnson, Lin. II. Title.
    BS2685.55.P37   2004
    227'.4'0071—dc22   2004005428

DONNA PARTOW is a Christian communicator with a compelling testimony of God's transforming power. Her uncommon transparency and passion for Christ have been used by God at women's conferences and retreats throughout North America. She is the bestselling author of numerous books and has been a popular guest on hundreds of radio and TV programs, including *Focus on the Family*.

If your church sponsors an annual women's conference or retreat, perhaps they would be interested in learning more about the author's special weekend programs. For more information, contact:

Donna Partow
Web site: *www.donnapartow.com*
E-mail: donnapartow@cox.net

LIN JOHNSON is managing editor of *The Christian Communicator, Advanced Christian Writer,* and *Church Libraries*. She has written over sixty books, specializing in Bible curriculum, and is a Gold Medallion Book Award recipient. Lin directs the Write-to-Publish Conference in the Chicago area and teaches at conferences across the country and internationally. She resides near Chicago. Her Web site is *www.wordprocommunications.com*.

Contents

Preface

Extracting the Precious Bible Study Series

This Bible study series began the day it finally dawned on me that there were two ways to learn the life lessons God has in store for us: the easy way and the hard way. Personally, I've always specialized in learning my lessons the hard way, through painful life experiences. Sure, I've learned a lot, but I've got the battle scars to prove it too. The easy way to learn is sitting at the feet of Jesus, meditating upon His Word. The longer I walk with God, the more determined I become to learn directly from Him—sitting quietly in the privacy of my prayer room rather than learning as I get jostled around out there in the cold, cruel world. Which way would you rather learn?

I used to think I was "getting away with something" when I neglected the spiritual disciplines such as prayer, Bible study, Scripture memorization, and participating in a small group study. But I was only deceiving myself. The plain and simple fact is this: We all reap what we sow. Nothing more, nothing less. God won't force you to study your Bible. He won't come down from heaven and clobber you over the head if you skip some of the questions in this book. He won't even be mad at you if you put this down right now and never pick it up again. In fact, God will love you the exact same amount. His unfailing love for you is completely unconditional.

But God's love doesn't wipe out the logical consequences of our choices. Here's how Deuteronomy 30:19–20 puts it:

> *This day I call heaven and earth as witnesses against*
> *you that I have set before you life and death, blessings*
> *and curses. Now choose life, so that you and your chil-*
> *dren may live and that you may love the Lord your God,*
> *listen to his voice, and hold fast to him.*

Reading God's Word is the ultimate choice for life, not only for us but to those who will come after us. Every moment we choose to spend searching, meditating, memorizing is a choice for life. Every moment we neglect His Word, we are choosing death—the death of our spiritual and personal potential; the death of an opportunity to become all God desires us to be. God's love is unconditional, but His blessings are not. Here's how the psalmist put it:

> *Blessed is the man*
> *who does not walk in the counsel of the wicked*
> *or stand in the way of sinners*
> *or sit in the seat of mockers.*
> *But his delight is in the law of the Lord,*
> *and on his law he meditates day and night.*
> *He is like a tree planted by streams of water,*
> *which yields its fruit in season*
> *and whose leaf does not wither.*
> *Whatever he does prospers.*
>
> —*Psalm 1:1–3*

God says we will be blessed (happy, fortunate, prosperous, and enviable) if we spend more time in His Word and less time with clueless people (my paraphrase). Does that mean we'll never have to learn anything the hard way? Not quite! Let's face it: Certain classes require a "hands-on" component. I couldn't graduate from chemistry class without stepping into the lab, putting on my scientist-wanna-be (or in my case, scientist-never-gonna-be) coat, and conducting some of those experiments for myself. At the same time, I found that my ability to conduct those experiments successfully was directly linked to the amount of time I spent studying the textbook in advance. You can't learn what it is to be a parent without having children underfoot. Neither can you fully comprehend God's faithfulness without finding yourself trapped in the middle of a real-world situation where nothing else can see you through. Nevertheless, there is much we *can* learn in solitude and study of God's Word so when we encounter various tests in life, we'll be well-prepared to experience a successful outcome.

Jeremiah 15:19 is a passage that has always been especially meaningful to me:

> *Therefore, thus says the Lord,*
> *"If you return, then I will restore you—*
> *Before Me you will stand;*
> *And if you extract the precious from the worthless,*
> *You will become My spokesman."*
> *—Jeremiah 15:19* NASB

The first time I heard those words, my heart leapt within me and I said, "Yes, Lord, I want to extract the precious from every worthless circumstance I must endure!" I was instantly overtaken with a holy determination to learn all I could from every class I landed in at the School of Hard Knocks.

Those of you who are familiar with my work know I've built my writing and speaking ministry on story illustrations and life lessons gleaned from my various follies and foibles. My friends all tease me whenever they see me embroiled in yet another mess, "Don't worry, Donna. You'll get through this . . . and turn it into a great illustration." And they're right! I always do. But with this new series, I wanted to do something entirely differ-ent. I wanted my readers to know that just as we can extract the precious from the worthless, we can extract the precious from the precious too! Rather than telling you my stories, I wanted you to read His story. You can learn to glean story illus-trations and life lessons while sitting peacefully at His feet rather than getting bloodied out in the street. Isn't that a beau-tiful thought?

The other thing I wanted to share with you is this: I love learning from other people, but I'd much rather learn from God. As much as I enjoy reading Christian books, completing various Bible studies, listening to teaching tapes, and attending conferences, nothing on earth compares to those moments when I realize God has cut out the middleman. When it's just Him, His Word, and me, He is serving as my personal tutor. That's when His Word truly comes alive for me. And that's what I want you to experience for yourself with the EXTRACTING THE PRECIOUS studies. I want to get out of the way as much as possible and let God teach you directly from His Word. You'll notice that I've saved my pithy little comments for the end of each chapter, so you aren't biased by my perspective on what's important. You can decide that for yourself.

USING THIS STUDY GUIDE

Every book in this series will feature twelve chapters, each of which is divided into three sections:

Search the Word features a series of inductive Bible study questions designed to help you interact with the Bible text. Use a Bible version that is easy to understand. I recommend the New International Version, but if you prefer a different version (e.g., New King James, New American Standard, *New Living*), that's fine. You may enjoy reading from several translations, and if you're a true scholar, the *Amplified Bible* is ideal for studying a passage in depth. You may want to complete each study in two or three sittings rather than answering all the questions at once. Then, instead of simply copying the Bible text, answer the questions in your own words.

Consider the Message provides a narrative section that illustrates the truth of the chapter, showing how it can be lived out in today's world.

Apply the Truth contains questions to help you apply the biblical teaching to your daily life, along with a verse or short passage to memorize. Depend on the Holy Spirit to guide and help you with these questions so He can pinpoint areas of your life where God wants you to practice His truth.

Although I suspect many of you will be using these books for your personal quiet time, I have included a brief Leader's Guide at the end of each book. It includes some background information on the Bible text, along with cross-references and suggestions for using this study guide in a group setting.

I want you to know how excited I am for you as you begin this journey with God and His Word. You will soon discover (if you don't know this already) that the truths you glean on your own will ultimately have far greater impact on your life than anything you've ever learned secondhand. People died to give us the right to study God's Word for ourselves. It's a great privilege. Make the most of it. As you do, here's my prayer for you:

> *For this reason I kneel before the Father, from whom his whole family in heaven and on earth derives its name. I pray that out of his glorious riches he may strengthen you with power through his Spirit in your inner being, so that Christ may dwell in your hearts through faith. And I pray that you, being rooted and established in love, may have power, together with all the saints, to grasp how wide and long and high and deep is the love of Christ, and to know this love that surpasses knowledge—that you may be filled to the measure of all the fullness of God.*
>
> *Now to him who is able to do immeasurably more than all we ask or imagine, according to his power that is at work within us, to him be glory in the church and in Christ Jesus throughout all generations, for ever and ever! Amen.*
>
> —*Ephesians 3:14–21*

Blessings,
His Vessel
Donna Partow

Introduction

Set Free to Live in Freedom

Once upon a time, I was a woman living in bondage. At first there was the bondage to other people's low opinion of me. My family went through an incredibly tough time during the Vietnam War era, and I spent many years in bondage to the painful memories of that period in our lives. Then there was my bondage to drugs. I literally couldn't make it past nine in the morning without getting high. I know that because a friend challenged me to do that simple thing. But I couldn't. I eventually became a drug dealer and did everything you might imagine a person will do to support a drug addiction.

Then I met and married a Middle Eastern man, born and raised in a Muslim culture. I spent twenty years in bondage to *his* bondage to a world view and a religious stronghold he couldn't overcome, even though he tried. I lived as a virtual hostage in my own home for many of those years, not permitted to leave my house without his permission and strict supervision. Not allowed to go for a walk around the block, not even allowed to sit on my front steps without his approval.

Yet of all the prison cells I've sat in (and I've been arrested, more than once by the way), none could compare to the prison of legalism. That's why the book of Galatians is so precious to me. Though I had read it many times in my dutiful annual trips through the Bible, I'll never forget the summer *it* read *me*. It was July 1999, and God had allowed me to come to the end of myself. Then He threw out a lifeline through the pages penned in frustration by the Apostle Paul, who said, "It is for freedom that Christ has set us free" (Galatians 5:1).

THE STORY BEHIND GALATIANS

Most people who are even remotely familiar with the Bible or the Christian faith know the apostle Paul was once a zealous Jew—one with formal training in the Law—and an active persecutor of Christians. We know of his famous Damascus Road experience, where he encountered Jesus, who completely turned his life around. After his conversion, Paul became the world's first missionary, taking the Good News about Jesus to non-Jews (Gentiles). He made three missionary journeys, risking his life to make disciples as he planted churches throughout the Roman Empire.

Some of those churches were in the province of Galatia, in modern-day Turkey. Paul established churches in the cities of Antioch, Iconium, Derbe, and Lystra during his first missionary journey (Acts 13:1–3, 13–14:20), then visited them again on later journeys (Acts 16:1–6; 18:23). The letter to the Christians in Galatia, written around A.D. 49, is the earliest of Paul's thirteen letters preserved in the New Testament.

Paul was no stranger to a good theological fight and this letter is prime evidence of that fact. The reader can plainly tell Paul is fighting mad. The issue at hand was the biggest controversy of Paul's day: whether or not Christians had to keep the Jewish Law. Having lived his entire life in bondage to the Law, Paul was determined to fight for Christian liberty.

Paul's passion for helping believers enjoy God's freedom shines through on every page of this book. It's not a dry doctoral thesis! And it's as pertinent today as it was back when Paul wrote it.

If you're longing to be set free from man-made rules about how to please God—if you want to discover instead joy and freedom in Christ—join me for a life-changing study. Once you've tasted the freedom God has for you, you'll never be the same.

Set Free by Good News

SEARCH THE WORD

1 What is the best news you've ever received?

How did it affect you?

In a world where bad news prevails (just listen to the nightly news for proof), good news is memorable. So when Paul wrote to the Galatians, he began his letter with the good news of salvation before mentioning the bad news he had to deal with.

Read verses 1-5.

2 Why did Paul introduce himself like this? *to show that his authority came from God, not man*

3 What do you learn about Christ from Paul's introduction?

He brings grace + peace
He gave Himself for our sins
He did so in obedience to the Father

4 What do you learn about God the Father?

It was His will to send Christ
gives grace + peace
He wants to deliver us from this
evil age; deliver us forever

any order or system ←

5 Why did Christ give himself for our sins?

to deliver us from
evil

The difficulty about salvation is not that we should be good enough to be saved, but that we should see that we are bad enough to need salvation.

-henrietta mears

Read verses 6-10.

6 Summarize the Galatians' problem that Paul had to deal with.

turning to a different
"gospel" - perverted gospel

7 What was his attitude toward the Galatians? Why?

He was astonished that
they had not remained true
to the true gospel

8 What does it mean to be "called . . . by the grace of Christ"?

through His sacrifice

9 Describe the standard by which the Galatians were to measure the gospel messages they heard.

what he had already preached to them

10 How do people "pervert the gospel" today?

by taking things out of context, by not considering the totality of Scripture

11 How did Paul emphasize the necessity of accurately telling the gospel?

"devote someone eternally to hell" accursed

12 Why is there a conflict between serving Christ by telling the truth and pleasing men?

men don't always want the truth. They want to serve themselves

13 What are some ways we struggle with this conflict today?

greed homosexuality pride acceptance of not "judging"

CONSIDER THE MESSAGE

The word *gospel* literally means "good news." What exactly is this good news, according to the Bible? Human beings no longer have any reason to believe they should try earning their way to heaven. Throughout the Old Testament period, people repeatedly tried—and always failed—to live up to God's holy standard. With the coming of Christ, God declared, "Stop trying. You are laboring in vain anyway. I simply wanted you to see your inability for yourselves. I wanted you to cry out to Me, so I could deliver you."

> When it comes to making up for our sin, God is no more impressed by our good deeds than He would be if we gave Him a basket full of dirty laundry. Nothing we can do is good enough for God. That's why we sinners—all of us—are powerless to save ourselves.
>
> —randy southern

The good news is that Jesus paid the penalty for our sins—and He paid it in full. Nothing we have ever done can make us less lovable to God, and nothing we might do in the future can make us more lovable. We are fully forgiven, fully loved. Not because of anything we have done or promised to do but because Jesus gave himself for us.

A free gift. A full pardon. That's good news.

But freebies make some people nervous. They think there must be a catch, a hidden agenda. Other people don't like feeling indebted; they'd rather earn their own way both *in* this world and *to* the next. After all, we often look down on "charity cases" and people who won't pay their own way. So it was in Paul's day. Certain people were uncomfortable with pure, unadulterated good news, so they added some bad news to it.

They told the Galatians, who were not Jewish, that if they really wanted to be saved, they needed Jesus *plus* some Jewish rituals. Jesus *plus* anything is always bad news.

This is the only letter in which Paul expresses no thanksgiving for the believers' faith and extends no commendation to the church. Even the Corinthians, who engaged in blatant sexual immorality, received words of encouragement for what they were doing right. But Paul had nothing good to say to those who were willing to buy into "Jesus Plus."

Paul also warns his readers against those who claim God has authorized them to institute Jesus Plus something or someone else. Islam and Mormonism, two of the fastest-growing world religions, were both founded by men who claimed an angel from heaven gave them a new revelation. In both cases, this new revelation represented a very different gospel—one based on works, not grace. Mormonism equals Jesus plus Joseph Smith plus works. Islam equals Jesus plus Mohammed plus the Five Pillars (works) of Islam. Paul's warning was not only for the Galatian church; it was a warning for all ages, including our own.

Later in this study we'll examine two counterfeits to freedom: legalism (living your life by the rule book) and license (throwing away the rule book). But here, right off the bat, Paul made it plain that legalism is more deadly, to be resisted more forcefully, than license. Jesus demonstrated the same truth when he said to the chief priests and the elders, "I tell you the truth, the tax collectors and the prostitutes are entering the kingdom of God ahead of you" (Matthew 21:32). Often it is easier for those living in obvious sin to recognize their need for a Savior. Yet the Bible says, "All have sinned and fall short of the glory of God" (Romans 3:23). Even the holiest person needs a Savior, because it takes only one sin to make a person a sinner. And sinners cannot stand in the presence of our Holy God.

APPLY THE TRUTH

1 Have you received Jesus' Good News gift of salvation by faith in Him alone? If so, what evidence can others see in your life? If not, talk with your group leader or a Christian friend about making this decision.

2 What specific steps can you take to be sure you don't follow another gospel? *Compare to Scripture*

3 Memorize Galatians 1:8:

> But even if we or an angel from heaven
> should preach a gospel other than the one we
> preached to you, let him be eternally con-
> demned!

Session Two
Galatians 1:11-24

Set Free by God's Call

SEARCH THE WORD

1 When has someone chosen you (e.g., for a team, a job, a ministry)?

How did being chosen make you feel?

We all like to be chosen, especially as opposed to being ignored or rejected. Paul knew what it was like to be chosen, hand-picked by God, as he reported in this section of Galatians.

Read verses 11-17.

2 How did Paul describe the gospel he preached?

3 What did Paul reveal about his life before God called him?

4 How did Paul's life and attitudes change when God called him?

5 How did Paul emphasize that his changed life and calling were from God, not anything he did?

> I am like a little pencil in God's hand. He does the writing. The pencil has nothing to do with it.
> –mother teresa

6 To what ministry did God call Paul?

7 What was Paul doing in Arabia for three years?

Read verses 18-24.

8 Why did Paul return to Jerusalem?

9 Why did he point out his limited contact with the other apostles?

10 What were people saying about Paul?

11 How do you think these remarks affected him?

> Once you are saved, God intends to use you for his goals. God has a *ministry* for you in his church and a *mission* for you in the world.
>
> –rick warren

12 What kind of impact did his transformed life have on others?

CONSIDER THE MESSAGE

Sometimes Christians sing beautiful songs that feature lovely sentiments but incorrect doctrine. At the risk of sounding like a nitpicker, I have a small problem with the old hymn "I Have Decided to Follow Jesus." I know what we mean when we sing it: We've decided to get up out of our chairs, pews, or what-have-yous. But that decision is always in response to what God has already done. In other words, if God hadn't tracked down your sorry you-know-what, you'd still be as lost as you ever were. If God hadn't pursued and irresistibly wooed you, deciding to follow Jesus would never have become a serious option.

> Whom wilt thou find
> to love ignoble thee,
> Save Me, save only Me?
> All which I took from thee,
> I did but take,
> Not for thy harms,
> But just that thou might'st
> seek it in My arms.
> All which thy child's mistake
> Fancies as lost, I have
> stored for thee at home:
> Rise, clasp My hand,
> and come!
>
> –francis thompson, excerpt from "The Hound of Heaven"

I once received an irate e-mail from a woman who objected to my use of the phrase "the hound of heaven," which I had borrowed from the nineteenth-century poem by Francis Thompson. She said something to the effect that "envisioning God as a drooling, sniffing hound was most unseemly." Indeed, the God of the universe sleeping in a stable surrounded by cow manure; stripped naked, publicly beaten, and paraded through the streets like a common criminal, hanging battered and bloody on a cross—are not all these equally "unseemly"? Yet God stooped down. And yes, I believe He daily stoops low enough to pursue the lost through alleyways, crack houses, and whorehouses. He found me, strung out on drugs, wallowing in my own vomit. Yes, He stoops. And I suspect that if His drooling would rescue one dying soul, Jesus would willingly drool.

Jesus made all of this perfectly clear: "You did not choose me, but I chose you" (John 15:16). Maybe I lack theological depth, but this statement strikes me as rather straightforward. It flies in the face of our democratic ideals, but the clear teaching of Scripture is that God chooses to set His love on certain people. Of all the nations on the earth, He chose Israel. Of all people on the earth, He chose you and me. I recently heard a prominent Bible teacher explain, "God chose those He knew in advance would choose Him." Popular, yes. Biblical? I'm not entirely sure. (Read Romans 8, 9, and 10.) If you're doing this study in a group, you can debate it for yourselves, as Christians have done for thousands of years. But you must promise to debate nicely and give each other freedom to examine God's Word and come to different conclusions.

As for me, I'm sitting here rejoicing in the thought that God handpicked me like He handpicked Paul. Paul didn't simply decide to follow Jesus. Jesus hunted him down on the Damascus Road and told him, "Now get up and go into the city, and you will be told what you must do" (Acts 9:6). God met me when I was sitting along a riverbank one day in July 1980. He didn't ask me if I wanted to follow Him. He told me to go and advance His Kingdom.

If you are a follower of Jesus Christ, I'm absolutely convinced it is because God handpicked you.

APPLY THE TRUTH

1 Paul had a clear sense of God's calling for both salvation and service. What is God calling you to do for His Kingdom?

2 How obedient have you been to God's call?

3 Thank God for handpicking you to follow Him, and ask for His help to obey His call for service.

4 Memorize Galatians 1:15–16:

> But when God, who set me apart from birth and called me by his grace, was pleased to reveal his Son in me so that I might preach him among the Gentiles, I did not consult any man.

Session Three
Galatians 2:1-10

Set Free to Proclaim the Gospel

SEARCH THE WORD

1 If someone were to follow you around for a week, what would that person hear you talk about the most?

politics / children's problems

What dominates our speech, as well as what dominates our checkbooks and time, indicates what's important to us. However, God didn't call us to major in the trivialities of life. He's put us where we're at for a reason, as Paul demonstrated in this section of Galatians.

Read verses 1-5.

2 Why did Paul return to Jerusalem?

He was told to by H.S. – to preach Gospel

Acts 15

3 Why was he so concerned about not requiring Gentile believers to become Jewish converts first?

its not the true gospell. Brings bondage

4 What are some ways we run "in vain"?

Of we are working outside of Gods will - even if we think we are working for Him

> This is the true joy in life, being used for a purpose recognized by yourself as a mighty one; being a force of nature instead of a feverish selfish little clod of ailments and grievances complaining that the world will not devote itself to making you happy.
> —george bernard shaw

5 How did the "false brothers," also called Judaizers, try to undermine Paul's ministry to the Gentiles?

said they had to be circumcised

6 What is the liberty those Judaizers wanted to take away?

freedom from the law?

7 How did Paul and the other leaders respond to those false teachers?

they did not yield

8 What is the "truth of the gospel" that Paul was so concerned about? *Christ died for uncircumcist as well as circum.*

9 How is it in danger today?

Read verses 6–10.

10 How was Paul's sphere of influence different from that of the other church leaders? *He preached to Gentiles*

> **The gospel is not something we go to church to hear; it is something we go from church to tell.**
> –vance havner

11 How did the leaders respond to Paul's call? *Right hand of fellowship*

12 What did they request that Paul and Barnabas do as they obeyed God's call to proclaim the Gospel to the Gentiles? *remember the poor*

Why do you think they made this request? *It was on their hearts*

13 How did Paul respond to the idea that some believers are more special than others? *God shows no favoratism*

> We need to recognize the fact that God calls people to different ministries in different places; yet we all preach the same Gospel and are seeking to work together to build His church.
>
> —warren w. wiersbe

CONSIDER THE MESSAGE

Anyone who pursues God does so for one reason only: God pursued first: "We love because he first loved us" (1 John 4:19). Your encounter may not have been as dramatic as Paul's or mine. For instance, my friend Glenda told me recently, "I always knew God was pursuing a relationship with me. Even as a little girl, I felt drawn to church, drawn to the Bible." For her, it was that simple. God was drawing her near. Perhaps you had a similar experience. The most saintly man I've ever known, missionary statesman Dr. William Miller, once shared with me that he could not point to a specific moment for his conversion. Instead, it was a gradual realization of God calling.

The question remains: Why? Why does God call us? Were there a few vacancies in the pews? Did God call you because you are so wonderful and He thought you might look good sitting in church? Many people act as if they believe John 15:16 says, "You did not choose me, but I chose you . . . to sit and make notes concerning what's wrong with everyone else." But that's not what it says. It says, "You did not choose me, but I chose you . . . to go." The call to each of us is to *go*, never to sit. God handpicked you because He has a specific assignment for you to fulfill on this planet. No one else can do it quite like you can. Like Paul, we are all given the task of proclaiming the Good News. Some proclaim it in words, others in song, still others through exemplary lives characterized by servanthood, not by rule-keeping.

According to E. M. Bounds, noted for his writings on the subject of prayer, "God has chosen to limit his actions on this earth to those things done in direct response to believing prayer." Why else would Jesus instruct us to *pray*, "Your kingdom come, your will be done on earth as it is in heaven" (Matthew 6:9–10)? If God's Kingdom was going to come and His will was going to be done whether or not we prayed, what would be the point of praying?

Have you ever had the experience of feeling prompted—even burdened—to pray for someone? I once read of a woman who woke in the middle of the night, impressed with the need to pray urgently for her daughter's safety. As it turns out, at that exact hour her daughter, a missionary in Africa, was in a stalled vehicle with her children—directly in the path of a stampeding elephant herd. Why did God bother to awaken this woman in the middle of the night *to pray*? Why not let her enjoy a good night's sleep and simply redirect the charging elephants *without* her prayer? Because "God has chosen to limit his actions on this earth to those things done in direct response to believing prayer." Our prayers truly make a difference.

God says, "I looked for a man among them who would build up the wall and stand before me in the gap on behalf of the land so I would not *have to* destroy it, but I found none" (Ezekiel 22:30, emphasis added). There's a spiritual battle being waged on this planet, and there are rules of engagement that God has apparently chosen to honor. One of those rules is that God generally will limit His actions on earth to those things that are accomplished in and through His people—specifically through the prayers of His people. Study the Bible. Study church history. There can be no doubt that almost every time God has chosen to intervene in the course of human events, He has chosen a man or a woman and given that person the assignment to carry out.

You were handpicked by God because there is work to be done, most of it on your knees. And He has chosen *you* to do it.

> So long as we imagine it is we who have to look for God, we must often lose heart. But it is the other way about—He is looking for us.
>
> —simon tuqwell

APPLY THE TRUTH

1 What sphere of influence has God given you?

2 How are you obeying His call to proclaim the Gospel in this sphere?

3 Ask God to use you in your sphere of influence this week without compromising the truth of the gospel.

4 Memorize Galatians 2:5:

> We did not give in to them [false teachers] for a moment, so that the truth of the gospel might remain with you.

Session Four
Galatians 2:11-21

Set Free by Grace Alone

SEARCH THE WORD

1 How do you usually react when someone wrongs you?

Cry

Why?

Most of us, if we're honest, want to punish people when they wrong us. But God didn't do that. He punished His Son instead. Paul often camped on that truth in his ministry; one of those times is recorded in this passage.

Read verses 11-13.

2 Who are the characters in this drama, and what did each of them do?

Peter - withrew fm Gentiles
Barnabas - carried away by Judaizers
hypocrisy
Paul - confronted Peter

3 Why did Peter act like this? *He didn't want to lose his standing w/ the Jews*

4 What were the consequences of his wrong actions?

led Barnabas astray

Every action of our lives touches on some chord that will vibrate in eternity.
–e. h. chapin

Read verses 14–16.

5 Why did Paul confront Peter publicly instead of privately?

6 What advice would Paul give today to Christians who are trying to impose legalistic demands on other believers?

Christ freed us from having to try to gain salvation through works

7 What is the bottom line of how we attain a right standing before God? *faith + Christ*

8 In what ways do we fall into the trap of trying to fulfill selected parts of the Old Testament Law?

Read verses 17–21.

9 What was the purpose of God's Law?

to show us we could not keep from sinning to pt out that we need a Savior

10 Instead of trying to keep the Law, Paul says we are "crucified with Christ." What does he mean by this statement?

we have victory over sin + death. old self is dead

What does justified mean? God credits to my account what Christ has done—just-as-if-I'd done it.
–henrietta mears

11 How does Christ live out His life through us?

indwelling of the H.S.

12 If keeping the Law could provide a right relationship with God, what would be unnecessary?

Christ's death

13 Why is it often easier or more attractive to live by rules than by faith?

You don't have to humble yourself you don't have to worry about disappointing God

God justifies sinners without justifying our sin.
-henrietta mears

CONSIDER THE MESSAGE

I was once asked to sum up my salvation experience within the allotted one-inch space on a preprinted form. I wrote: "Saved by the blood of Jesus in July 1980. Been justified. Being sanctified. Will someday be glorified."

It is vitally important for Christians to understand these three central doctrines of the faith: justification, sanctification, and glorification. The book of Galatians sets forth the case for justification by faith alone with compelling clarity. When we place our faith in Jesus, we are instantly declared justified, or acquitted in God's sight. Jesus takes our "guilty" verdict and transfers His "not guilty" verdict to us. Our sin is no longer held against us, and we are granted entrance into heaven. This legal transaction is an established fact. A done deal.

It is on that basis alone that we will one day stand before God's throne and be transformed into His likeness—our glorification (1 John 3:2). But in between what happened on the day of your salvation and what will happen one glorious day, the process of working out that salvation takes place. That process is sanctification.

For many years I was puzzled by the verse, "Work out your salvation with fear and trembling" (Philippians 2:12). I knew we could not earn our salvation, so what were we supposed to work on? Once I learned the distinction between the soul and spirit, suddenly the passage made sense. It means to take what God has already accomplished in our spirits and let it transform our soul—our mind, will, and emotion. Yes, God has made it possible for us to enjoy heaven in heaven, but we can also enjoy a little of heaven down here on earth. How? By cooperating with God as He transforms us from the inside out.

Justification is not a ticket to sin. It's an invitation to pursue holiness.

Christians in some churches today overlook the significance of our justification—our secure position in Christ—and become obsessed with the pursuit of sanctification. Their Christianity then becomes performance oriented and legalistic. They place great emphasis on outward conformity, with little concern for the inward reality and *no* concern for love or mercy toward those who don't measure up to the church's exacting standards.

Others misuse verses about our justification to obliterate the need for our active participation in sanctification. The result is license and worldliness. These churches preach grace, grace, and more grace. They preach the effectiveness of the Cross, that Christ has done it all. And we *should* preach such messages, because they are doctrinally correct. However, we often fail to mention that "a man is a slave to whatever has mastered him" (2 Peter 2:19b). We are free to live however we choose, but we are not free from the consequences of those choices.

As we study passages from God's Word, let's be sure to keep them in context. Is the passage addressing our position? Is it a truth to claim? To be more theological about it, does it refer to our justification? Or is it addressing our journey? Is it a lifestyle to pursue? Back to theological terms: Is it written in regard to our sanctification?

Understanding this distinction can help us approach the Christian life in a healthy, balanced way, as Paul urged the Galatians to do.

APPLY THE TRUTH

1 On what have you been depending to live a life pleasing to God? *forgiveness*

An understanding of how grace and personal, vigorous effort work together is essential for a lifelong pursuit of holiness.

–jerry bridges

2 How does your answer compare with Paul's teaching in this passage?

3 What changes could you make to "live by faith in the Son of God"?

4 Memorize Galatians 2:20–21:

> I have been crucified with Christ and I no longer live, but Christ lives in me. The life I live in the body, I live by faith in the Son of God, who loved me and gave himself for me. I do not set aside the grace of God, for if righteousness could be gained through the law, Christ died for nothing!

Session Five
Galatians 3:1-14

Set Free From the Requirements of the Law

SEARCH THE WORD

1 Rate your attitude toward rules by drawing an X in the appropriate spot on the following graph:

| . . . . |

I never keep rules.   *I always keep rules.*

Explain your attitude.

When it comes to keeping rules, most of us fall somewhere between these two extremes, whether it's in the middle or closer to one statement or the other. But when it comes to rule-keeping and salvation, there is no middle ground, as Paul pointed out in this section of Galatians.

Read verses 1-5.

2 What was Paul's main concern for the Galatian believers?

3 What progression do you notice in the questions Paul asked?

4 How do these questions relate to Christ's death?

> There are *no* conditions for acceptance with God apart from surrender to Christ and life in the Spirit.
>
> –scot mcknight

Read verses 6-9.

5 How did Abraham attain his right standing before God?

6 How does Paul's teaching differ from what the Galatians were hearing from false teachers? (See 2:1–5.)

7 Why was this example of Abraham a powerful one in Paul's argument against the necessity of keeping the Law for right standing before God?

Read verses 10-14.

8 What is the result of relying on works instead of faith for salvation?

9 Summarize Paul's argument against keeping the Law for salvation.

> The law deals with what we are and do, while grace deals with what Christ is and does.
> –henrietta mears

10 What are some evidences that a Christian is relying on "observing the law" today?

11 How did Christ's death free us from trying to work for our salvation?

12 What are the benefits of placing our faith in Christ alone?

CONSIDER THE MESSAGE

God has always offered human beings options, even from the earliest days in the Garden of Eden. He told Adam and Eve, "If you want to partake of the tree of life, I offer it to you freely. If you'd rather do things your way, deciding for yourself what is good and evil, you're on your own." (See Genesis 2:16–17.) He told the Israelites over and over again, "Choose life or death" (Deuteronomy 30:1–20).

When Nicodemus approached Jesus in humility, inquiring what he must do to be saved, Jesus told him everyone who simply believes will have eternal life. "Be born again," Jesus said. Start all over like a little child who doesn't claim to know it all. Yet when the rich young ruler approached Jesus, asking the same question, he got a completely different answer. Jesus told him to sell everything he had and give it to the poor (Matthew 19:16–24).

One was offered a free gift; the other was required to make what he would consider the ultimate sacrifice. Why such different responses? Because Jesus meets people where they are. To those seeking grace, he offers grace. To those smug, self-congratulatory people who think they can earn their way to heaven, Jesus demands flawless adherence to the letter of the Law. (Imagine the nerve of the rich young ruler claiming he had always loved his neighbor as himself. Please!)

To the woman caught in the act of adultery, Jesus said, "Neither do I condemn you" (John 8:11). To the five-times divorced Samaritan woman at the well, Jesus revealed himself as the Messiah and offered her living water (John 4:7–26). Yet when the Pharisees, who claimed to flawlessly uphold the Law, came inquiring about the issue of divorce, Jesus made the Law even more stringent than Moses had (Matthew 19:3–10). He told the Pharisees that if they so much as *looked* at a woman lustfully, they were guilty of adultery (Matthew 5:28). Name one man who can claim "not guilty" to that one!

Basically, Jesus turned the situation on its head. The Pharisees wanted to know what loophole in the Law would allow men to divorce their wives "for any and all reasons." Jesus said, "Adultery is the only real reason to divorce and you are *all* guilty" of adultery. No wonder they hated Jesus! But wait a minute: Why didn't Jesus spell out laws about divorce and remarriage to the Samaritan woman? To those seeking grace, He offers grace. To those who want to fulfill the Law, He gives them the Law to the nth degree.

It's up to you. Grace. Or Law. You get to pick. But what God will not tolerate is a mix-and-match approach. The grace-and-Law combo is not on the menu here. That's the whole point of Galatians. If you miss that, you've missed everything. Which will you choose? Just be forewarned: If you choose *law*—that is, if you want to try earning your own way to heaven—you can't make even one mistake! Not ever! May I make a suggestion, friend-to-friend? Choose grace!

APPLY THE TRUTH

1 What spiritual goals are you trying to attain by keeping rules in your own effort?

> To the legalist, Jesus presents a God of unbending, righteous demands. To the sinner, Christ freely offers forgiveness and restoration.
>
> –dr. gary kinnaman

2 How can you cooperate with the Holy Spirit instead of striving in your own strength?

3 Ask God to help you rely on the Spirit's power—rather than your own strength or rule-keeping ability—so you can grow in the grace and knowledge of God.

4 Memorize Galatians 3:14:

> **He redeemed us in order that the blessing given to Abraham might come to the Gentiles through Christ Jesus, so that by faith we might receive the promise of the Spirit.**

Session Six
Galatians 3:15-25

Set Free to Enjoy an Inheritance

SEARCH THE WORD

1 If you could choose your own inheritance, what would it be?

Why?

Wouldn't it be great to know you were going to inherit whatever you want? Unfortunately, inheritances rarely work that way. But God has promised us an inheritance greater than any we could dream up, as Paul explained in this passage.

Read verses 15-18.

2 What inheritance did God promise Abraham? (Read Genesis 12:1–3.)

3 In what ways did Paul contrast God's covenant promise with the Law?

4 Why couldn't the Law change the covenant promise God gave Abraham?

5 What is the inheritance God has promised us? (See also Ephesians 1:3–14.)

Read verses 19-25.

6 What was the purpose of the Law?

7 For how long was the Law intended to be in effect?

8 Why did it require a mediator?

9 Who is the mediator Paul referred to in these verses? (See 1 Timothy 2:5.)

10 Why did God give both the Law and covenant promises?

> For above all else, the Christian life is a love affair of the heart. It cannot be lived primarily as a set of principles or ethics. It cannot be managed with steps and programs. It cannot be lived exclusively as a moral code leading to righteousness.
>
> –brent curtis & john eLdredge

11 How does a life lived according to the Law differ from a life lived by faith in God?

CONSIDER THE MESSAGE

An inheritance is something we get for free—just because of who our relatives are. Then we get to spend it! We cannot earn an inheritance. It is freely given.

When do we receive an inheritance? When we die? Or when our benefactor dies? The answer, of course, is when our benefactor dies. Jesus has already died, so we can receive our spiritual inheritance now. The Scripture says, "We *are* heirs—heirs of God and co-heirs with Christ" (Romans 8:17, emphasis added). It doesn't say that someday we *will be*; we already *are*.

God "has blessed us [past tense] in the heavenly realms with every spiritual blessing" and has given us the Holy Spirit as "a deposit guaranteeing our inheritance" (Ephesians 1:3, 14).

While it is obvious that there is much more to come in heaven, God intends for us to experience the privileges of a coheir *now*. As Psalm 23:5 says, "You prepare a table before me in the presence of my enemies." Where are our enemies? Are they in heaven? No, they're right here on earth. God wants to set a table of blessing before us here and now.

Of course, while it's true that an inheritance is a free gift, we've all heard stories of people who squander their inherited wealth or who do not value it. Even though we don't do anything to deserve an inheritance, we must take action to preserve it.

How valuable is the spiritual heritage you have been given? Maybe it was passed down to you by your parents or grandparents. Maybe your family has passed down a godly heritage for generations to the point that you take it for granted. You may recall Esau, who sold his birthright for a bowl of stew (Genesis 25:29–34; Hebrews 12:16). He simply saw no value for it. Sadly, he realized too late that he should have placed a higher value on what his father had to offer him. Let's not make that same mistake.

One more question: What exactly is our inheritance? First Peter 2:5 describes believers as "a holy priesthood." Throughout the Old Testament, God reminded the Israelites that the priests were not to be given land as an inheritance, as the rest of the tribes were. Instead, the Lord said, "'I am to be the only inheritance the priests have'" (Ezekiel 44:28). No real estate on earth can compare with the inheritance we have been given: the right to have a personal relationship with our heavenly Father.

And with that inherited position comes the privilege to "approach the throne of grace with confidence, so that we may receive mercy and find grace to help us in our time of need" (Hebrews 4:16). Under Old Testament Law, only the high priest could enter into God's presence; and he could do so only once a year on Yom Kippur, the Day of Atonement (Hebrews 9:7). Since we are not only priests but daughters and sons, we can enter into God's presence freely whenever we want. We have the privilege of interceding, not just for ourselves, but for others, as well.

In addition to full access to the Father while we are on earth, Jesus is also storing up for us "an inheritance that can never perish, spoil or fade—kept in heaven for you" (1 Peter 1:4). We can't even imagine what those riches might be because "no eye has seen, no ear has heard, no mind has conceived what God has prepared for those who love him" (1 Corinthians 2:9).

What could be more valuable than a free gift like that? Don't squander it or trade it away cheap. Or, like Esau, you will someday regret it (Hebrews 12:17). Instead, live a life of service and gratitude because you have the greatest inheritance possible.

APPLY THE TRUTH

1 In what ways are you trying to earn your inheritance by keeping rules, especially man-made ones?

2 How can you develop a heart of gratitude for your spiritual inheritance and God's promises?

3 Memorize Galatians 3:18:

> For if the inheritance depends on the law,
> then it no longer depends on a promise; but
> God in his grace gave it to Abraham through a
> promise.

Set Free to Live As Children of God

SEARCH THE WORD

1 If you could choose your family, whom would you choose?

Why?

Most of us have wished we belonged to a different family at least once, usually when we were punished as children, denied the right to do something as teens, or dealing with wacky relatives as adults. But we don't get to choose our families; we're born into them or perhaps marry into them. In the spiritual realm, God has chosen us to be part of His family. That family relationship creates both challenges and opportunities, as Paul described in this section of Galatians.

Read 3:26-29.

2 How did Paul describe the family to which the Galatians belonged?

Sons of God through faith in Jesus Christ / We've put on Christ / Abraham's seed

3 How does our oneness as children of God affect our differences that Paul mentioned here?

minimizes them

> **One of the tragedies of legalism is that it gives the appearance of spiritual maturity when, in reality, it leads the believer back into a "second childhood" of Christian experience.**
>
> –warren w. wiersbe

4 In what practical ways can we demonstrate this oneness?

Believers have a special bond that transcends race gender social status

5 What does it mean to be Abraham's seed and "heirs according to the promise"?

God's promises to Abraham are ours – heirs of His spiritual blessing – justification by faith

Read 4:1-7.

6 In what ways is a childish person like a slave?

obey rules set out for you

7 How is living under the Law to gain a right standing with God a sign of immaturity?

obey rules outwardly

More than anything else, perhaps, this is the distinguishing mark of genuine Christian faith; we are given the privilege of calling God "Father." We enter into His presence in the consciousness that we belong, and are at home with Him.

—sinclair b. ferguson

8 In what ways are we like slaves before we become children of God?

As sinners, w/o Him, the only thing we could do was try to obey the law

9 How did Jesus satisfy the Law's requirements to free us from being slaves?

He was the perfect, sinless sacrifice

10 What are the "full rights of sons" that Jesus offers us through faith in Him?

freedom from the law, salvation, right to be His child

11 What benefits of being a child of God did Paul mention here?

God's heir to call him abba

12 How does it feel to be a son instead of a slave?

Can go to Him anytime. = to be loved

CONSIDER THE MESSAGE

In the late 1990s, I met a family who had fallen on hard times after the sudden death of the father. They lived in a cold climate, yet their modest cabin in the mountains had no heating system other than a large fireplace in the living room. The mother would wake up throughout the night to put wood on the fire to keep her children from freezing. Though she worked hard to keep the family together, you could tell she was under tremendous strain. They seemed "down on their luck" if you can picture what I mean.

> The biblical measure of spiritual maturity is not how long we've been saved or how many spiritual things we've done. Instead, it is determined by how much more like Christ we are today than we were two months ago. God takes pleasure in our lives as we grow to be more like Christ, but to become more like Him we must change—first in the way we think and then in the way we act.
>
> –joseph m. stowell

For several years, I stayed in close contact with the family, assisting them whenever I could. Then I discovered an amazing bit of information: the father had left behind a trust fund worth millions of dollars. So why were his children living in dire circumstances? Because the trust fund had been set up in such a way that the money can do them no good until they grow up.

Our Heavenly Father has given us a rich inheritance—indeed "every spiritual blessing." But it won't do us any good until we GROW UP. Too many Christians are childish. Yes, they are *children* of God, but at some point we need to become God's grown-up sons and daughters.

Children need a baby-sitter (the Bible says that's exactly what the Old Testament law was—a baby-sitter). They need someone to order their steps and tell them what to do. But a mature adult has learned to govern her own behavior. Her actions are a reflection not of her parent's rules, but of the priorities she has learned and adopted as her own. For example, I no longer go to bed at a specific time because I *have to;* I choose to get a reasonable amount of sleep because it is wise. Nor do I eat healthy food because *my mom said so;* I choose to eat right because I'm mindful that my body is the temple of the Holy Spirit. A child and an adult may be eating the exact same food at the dinner table: one under outer compulsion, the other based on inner conviction. God wants us to live according to Bible-based, Holy Spirit-inspired convictions; not a set of rules being enforced by your unfriendly local church.

Another childish thing many Christians do is compare ourselves to one another. This is so unwise! My parents had eight children and we are all completely different; the same is true in the family of God. Comparison leads to nothing but sibling rivalry and heartache. I had one sister in Christ I was insanely jealous of, because it looked like God was pitching a party for her rather than me. One day, when I was stewing in my kitchen, God paid me a little visit. Now God does not routinely have audible conversations with me, but when He speaks, I know it's Him. I find that He usually speaks Scripture. This is what He said to me: "My child, you are always with me and everything I have is yours."

These are the words the Father had spoken to the *older brother* in the parable of the prodigal son (Luke 15:31). I think what God was trying to say to me was: Why are you acting like some underprivileged child? I have given you everything you need, but it's not doing you one drop of good because you're such a baby! It's time to grow up!

Is it time for you to grow up? Is it time to leave behind the baby-sitters and sibling rivalry, and learn to live as an adult child of the richest Father in the Universe? He has given you everything you need; all you have to do is open your eyes and see the truth.

APPLY THE TRUTH

1 How have you behaved like a childish slave this past week?

2 How have you behaved like an adult child of God this past week?

3 Thank God for welcoming you into His family and for the benefits that come with that relationship. Ask Him to help you behave like an adult instead of a child this week.

4 Memorize Galatians 4:1 and 7:

> What I am saying is that as long as the heir
> is a child, he is no different from a slave,
> although he owns the whole estate. . . .
> So you are no longer a slave, but a son;
> and since you are a son, God has made you
> also an heir.

Session Eight
Galatians 4:8-20

Set Free Never to Be Enslaved Again

SEARCH THE WORD

1 In what ways have you been a slave to someone or something other than Christ?

How did that "slavery" affect your relationship with God?

It's easy to let someone else do our thinking for us. Or to let things such as materialism or bad habits, like gluttony, take over our lives. Without realizing it, we can slip into slavery, including some forms of Christianity that set rules above relationship. That's what Paul was dealing with when he wrote to the Galatian believers.

Read verses 8-11.

2 To what had the Galatians been enslaved?

3 How did they escape from this bondage?

> **Often we do not enjoy our freedom in Christ because we are afraid of what others will think. We do or don't do certain things because of a fear that we will be judged or gossiped about by others. But standing firm in our freedom in Christ means we resist the urge to live by the fear of what others think.**
>
> –jerry bridges

4 What "weak and miserable principles" were the Galatians turning back to?

5 In what ways have contemporary Christians turned back to "weak and miserable principles"?

6 Why do you think Christians are so easily pressured into legalistic living of do's and don'ts, special days, etc.?

7 Why would Paul's efforts be wasted because the Galatians were observing special religious days and Jewish rituals?

Read verses 12–20.

8 How did Paul's relationship with the Galatians begin?

9 How did their treatment of Paul change? Why?

> Those who seek to please God only are invincible from within. Not only that, but when we stop striving to please people, we are also unintimidated from without.
>
> –charLes swindoLL

10 What is the connection between "weak and miserable principles" and losing joy?

11 When have you observed this connection in your life or the lives of other Christians?

12 How did Paul's behavior differ from that of the false teachers who were trying to drag the Galatians away from their freedom in Christ?

13 What is so dangerous about the situation Paul described in verse 17?

14 How can we guard against it?

15 How did Paul express his love and concern for the Galatian believers?

16 Why was he so perplexed about the Galatians?

CONSIDER THE MESSAGE

If we learn anything at all from the story of the Israelites, we realize that being set free from bondage is one thing; learning to live in freedom is another trip entirely. Time after time, they looked back to Egypt. Sure, it was a land of slavery, but hey, the food wasn't all that bad (Numbers 11:5)! They longed for the familiar and conveniently forgot how they had cried out to God to deliver them from their misery.

Here in Galatians, Paul echoes Moses' frustrations as he led the Israelites. Why on earth would someone want to turn back to slavery? Why would they want someone else to tell them exactly what to do—when, how, and why to do it? Why? Because people are often like sheep. They like to be herded so they don't have to think or choose for themselves. I'm continually amazed at the number of Christians who want to live according to a list of rules. Rather than looking to God, they look to any authoritative figure who rises up and calls himself a spiritual leader. They *want* someone else to tell them exactly what to do.

Even though the Bible says "we are not under law but under grace" (Romans 6:15), Christians still like to make up laws. People invariably choose those laws they feel confident they can adhere to, then build an entire theology around them. Laws about dress codes, music, movies, dancing, dietary restrictions, the Sabbath, and even hairstyles. Ironically, I am familiar with two Christian sects that have rules about men's facial hair: one group will throw you out if you *have* facial hair; the other will throw you out if you *don't*. Go figure!

I once attended a church with very strict laws about the Sabbath. You couldn't go out to lunch after the service; you couldn't even buy a gallon of milk. Some went so far as to say you had to do all your cooking the night before and leave the dishes until Monday. I was a college student at the time and remember living in emotional torment every Sunday because I wasn't allowed to study—and felt tremendously guilty if I broke the rules.

Now, don't get me wrong. I still believe that observing a Sabbath—setting aside one day per week to focus on our spiritual lives—is a wonderful principle. However, we are not constrained by Old Testament restrictions because Christ himself *is* our Sabbath rest (Hebrews 4:1–11). It is in Him, daily, that we receive spiritual refreshment. It is *to* Him, daily, that we should withdraw from the cares of this world to find rest for our souls.

Nor do I have a problem with Christian modesty until it goes too far. I once knew a teenage girl who walked into a church, desperate for help. A middle-aged woman (no doubt a pillar in the church) rushed over—but not to greet her. Oh, no! She was anxious to tell this troubled teen to *leave* because "we don't allow women to wear pants in this church." I'm sure she returned to her pew and congratulated herself for upholding God's righteous standards with never a thought of the devastated teenager walking home alone.

Talk about "weak and miserable principles." How many people are turned away from churches because they aren't adhering to whatever set of laws that particular church has enthroned? Indeed, this is what Jesus condemned the Pharisees for doing: "They tie up heavy loads and put them on men's shoulders, but they themselves are not willing to lift a finger to move them" (Matthew 23:4). How do you know when your perfectly good principle has turned into a law? Simple: When you use it as a tool to judge other people or as a measure of your own righteousness.

Although it is wonderful to live your life according to certain Christian principles, principles are not more important than people. People are more important than principles. You can search the entire Gospel record and not find a single instance where Jesus elevated principles above people. Let's follow His lead, rather than "weak and miserable principles."

APPLY THE TRUTH

1 What enslaving former habits—spiritual and physical—are you tempted to go back to?

> When you are rightly related to God, it is a life of freedom and liberty and delight, you *are* God's will, and all your commonsense decisions are His will for you unless He checks.
> —oswaLd chambers

Why?

2 How can you guard against being enslaved in these ways again?

3 What will your life look like if you live in freedom instead of slavery?

4 Memorize Galatians 4:9:

> But now that you know God—or rather are known by God—how is it that you are turning back to those weak and miserable principles? Do you wish to be enslaved by them all over again?

Session Nine
Galatians 4:21-31

Set Free by a Promise

SEARCH THE WORD

1 What advantages does a firstborn child have?

If you're a firstborn, you probably enjoyed some privileges the rest of your siblings didn't. Or if you're not, you may have been jealous of how your oldest brother or sister was treated. It was no different in Abraham's family, as you'll discover in this section of Galatians.

Read verses 21-27.

2 What did Paul ask the Galatians to think about?

Why?

3 Why did Paul bring Abraham into this discussion?

4 Why was Isaac, the son by the free woman, more special than Ishmael, the son by the slave woman?

> **Salvation is the beginning, not the ending. After we are born, we must grow (1 Peter 2:2; 2 Peter 3:18). Along with maturity comes weaning: we must lay aside "childish things" (1 Cor. 13:11). How easy it is for us to hold the "toys" of our earlier Christian days and fail to lay hold of the "tools" of the mature believer.**
>
> –warren w. wiersbe

5 What was the promise that Isaac was the result of? (Also read Genesis 17:15–22.)

6 What covenants do Hagar, the slave woman, and Sarah, the free woman, represent?

7 What are the differences between these two covenants?

8 How does this analogy of the two women and covenants aid in understanding Law and grace, slavery and freedom?

Read verses 28-31.

9 In what ways were the Galatian believers like Isaac?

10 How was the legalists' opposition to the Galatian Christians like Ishmael's persecution of Isaac?

11 Why couldn't Ishmael share Abraham's inheritance with Isaac?

12 What change in spiritual direction did Paul want the Galatians to make?

Why?

> The truth of the gospel is intended to free us to love God and others with our whole heart. When we ignore this heart aspect of our faith and try to live out our religion solely as correct doctrine or ethics, our passion is crippled, or perverted, and the divorce of our soul from the heart purposes of God toward us is deepened.
>
> –brent curtis & john eldredge

CONSIDER THE MESSAGE

Throughout most of my Christian life, I have lived like a child of the slave woman. Whenever I put forth effort toward my spiritual growth, my approach was to study (dissect would be a more accurate term) Scripture, read books, listen to tapes, attend conferences, etc., all with a view toward increasing my knowledge about God. And because I was a diligent student, I learned lots of doctrine and guidelines and rules for Christian living.

Yet despite my vast storehouse of information, I was *not* becoming more like Jesus. In fact, quite the opposite was true. I was becoming a rigid, legalistic jerk. It was a long road, but I finally came to the place where I recognized that all my good doctrine had managed to accomplish was to transform me into the kind of person Jesus wouldn't want to spend time with.

God's Word is supposed to be like our daily bread, giving nourishment to our soul. But I treated it like bubble gum instead. Gum is great for blowing bubbles and performing tricks to impress other people, but it never seeps down into your body to become part of the fabric of your being. I knew I was enslaved to my chewing-gum approach to Christianity, but I didn't know how to break free. You might say I was stuck!

Perhaps you've fallen into the same trap. Knowledge about

God is not a substitute for a relationship with God. The issue is never: Am I learning more about God? It is always: Am I becoming more like Him? Unfortunately, I used my list of rules and set of beliefs as a tool to evaluate other people. If they didn't follow the rules or believe the right things, I wrote them off. The more rules I uncovered, the more so-called "truths" I learned, the shorter my list of "approved people" became. The frightening part is that there are literally hundreds of thousands of people who believe this approach to Christianity is pleasing to God.

But the child of the free woman lives on bread, not chewing gum. Bread journeys through your internal system and changes you from the inside out. We've already seen that the Law doesn't bring life, so how do we draw life-giving sustenance from God's Word? I'm convinced it is in meditating on God's promises. As we consider all God has done for us, our hearts begin to overflow with gratitude. We will begin to offer others the same grace God has extended to us. We will become grateful, thankful people.

Outwardly, in terms of behavior, our lives may look the same whether we're living on spiritual chewing gum or bread. Inwardly, bread makes all the difference. This explains why one Christian may grow weary while another serves with joy. One is malnourished; the other is well fed. Paul addresses this issue again in Colossians 2:6–8: "So then, just as you received Christ Jesus as Lord, continue to live in him, rooted and built up in him, strengthened in the faith as you were taught, and overflowing with thankfulness. See to it that no one takes you captive through hollow and deceptive philosophy, which depends on human tradition and the basic principles of this world rather than on Christ."

Let's live as children of the free woman. Let's leave behind Christian servitude and discover the joy of Christian gratitude.

APPLY THE TRUTH

1 What does being a child of the promise mean to you?

> The old nature loves legalism, because it gives the old nature a chance to "look good." ... The Christian who claims to be spiritual because of what he doesn't do is only fooling himself. It takes more than negations to make a positive, fruitful spiritual life.
>
> —warren w. wiersbe

2 Which of your standards for living the Christian life do you try to impose on others?

3 In light of this passage, what changes do you need to make in your expectations about how Christians are to live?

4 Memorize Galatians 4:31:

> Therefore, brothers, we are not children of the slave woman, but of the free woman.

Session Ten
Galatians 5:1-15

Set Free to Love Others

SEARCH THE WORD

1 If you were free to do anything you wanted, how would your life be different?

Most of us chafe under restrictions we don't like; we long for more freedom. But when it comes to our spiritual lives, we gravitate toward living under more rules and regulations than God intended for us, which is not a new problem. In fact, Paul addressed this issue in Galatians 5.

Read verses 1-6.

2 What challenge did Paul give the Galatian believers?

Why?

> Despite God's call to be free and His earnest admonition to resist all efforts to curtail it, there is very little emphasis in Christian circles today on the importance of Christian freedom. Just the opposite seems to be true. Instead of promoting freedom, we stress our rules of conformity. Instead of preaching living by grace, we preach living by performance. Instead of encouraging new believers to be conformed to Christ, we subtly insist that they be conformed to our particular style of Christian culture.
>
> –jerry bridges

3 What did it cost Christ to give us this freedom? (See also 1 Peter 1:18–19.)

4 What is the "yoke of slavery" Paul warned against? (For background, read Acts 15:1, 5–10.)

5 If the Galatians were to go back to this yoke, what would be the results?

6 What are some of the yokes of slavery contemporary Christians try to put on others?

7 How do we fall away from grace?

8 Why is "faith expressing itself through love" the only thing that counts?

Read verses 7–12.

9 How did the Galatians get detoured from the Christian race they were running?

> **Love God, and do whatever you want.**
> –st. augustine

10 Next Paul switched to a cooking metaphor. Why did he use the analogy of yeast to describe the situation in the Galatian church?

11 How did Christ's cross end the Law with its rules and regulations for pleasing God?

12 Why was Paul so angry at the Judaizers, the Christians who wanted everyone to keep the Jewish Law?

Read verses 13–15.

13 What limitation did Paul put on the freedom we have in Christ?

I like the way some saint of old once put it: "Love God with all your heart ... then do as you please." The healthy restraint is in the first phrase, the freedom is in the second. That's how to live a grace-oriented, liberated life.
  –charLes r. swindoLL

14 In contrast, how should we use our freedom?

15 What does "biting and devouring" look like?

CONSIDER THE MESSAGE

Is the contemporary American church making itself too attractive to the lost? That's the topic I recently debated with a friend whom I hold in the highest regard—even though we sharply disagree on this issue. For two solid hours we argued over "the offense of Starbucks coffee and Krispy Kreme doughnuts." Though she had lived in one of the largest cities in America for more than a year, she had not yet settled into a home church. There was something troubling at every one she visited. Two pastors wore inappropriate clothing; another told an inappropriate joke. The music wasn't right at four churches, and one performed a drama that wasn't scripturally accurate. Still another had an unusual seating arrangement. Several churches gave her presents, in addition to free coffee and doughnuts—

and she found that rather strange.

My humble opinion? I don't think God is all that picky about clothing styles, seating arrangements, and such—as long as people are serving Him with sincerity. I would have enjoyed the free coffee and doughnuts—and there's nothing I love more than presents!

I recently met a woman whose mother went to the Salvation Army every day during the Depression. You'll never guess why! Yep, they were giving away free coffe and doughnuts. That woman became a Christian and raised two Christian daughters, one of whom is Captain Karen Humphreys of the Salvation Army. Karen and her sister have now carried the legacy to the next generation, having raised several Christian children of their own. Ah, the miracle-working power of coffee and doughnuts . . . when given in Jesus' name!

My friend's final concern haunts me most: "We are losing sight of the fact that the gate is narrow." I was blown away. There are currently over six billion, three hundred million people on the planet. I've decided to write out the zeros so we can all see them for ourselves. That's over 6,300,000,000 people. Most of these people will never see the gospel lived out before them in any credible way. These are real people, my friends. People with families. People with thoughts, feelings, hopes, and dreams, just like you and me. People in danger of spending eternity separated from God.

I could be wrong, of course, but here's what I told my friend: It seems to me that even if a few hundred thousand Americans slip in through the gate sipping Starbucks, the gate is *still* narrow. But it's almost like some Christians cherish the thought that "broad is the road that leads to destruction" (Matthew 7:13). That way they can congratulate themselves on being part of an exclusive group. You know why it offends us that people are entering the Kingdom without having their theological ducks in a row? Without living up to the exacting standards we've set for ourselves? Because doing so lowers our status. If any old person can just walk off the street, grab a doughnut, and get into the Kingdom, our country club loses a little of its glitter.

This is *exactly, exactly, exactly* why the Jewish leaders despised—and ultimately murdered—Jesus. He was letting five thousand people at a time sneak into the Kingdom munching loaves and fishes. Outrageous! It's *exactly* why the Judaizers followed Paul around, meddling in every church he planted. In essence, they said to Paul, "How dare you make it easy on people when we are making it so hard on ourselves! It's not fair. If we're going to be miserable following God, no one is going to claim to follow Him while still having a good time."

That is the "offense of the cross." It hasn't lessened to any extent in two thousand years. I'm certain it never will.

> Don't get impatient with others. Remember how God dealt with you—with patience and with gentleness.
> –oswald chambers

APPLY THE TRUTH

1 How has the freedom you have in Christ had an impact on your life?

2 How can you stand firm in that freedom this week?

3 How can you balance your freedom in Christ with heart obedience to Him and love for others?

4 Memorize Galatians 5:1:

> **It is for freedom that Christ has set us free. Stand firm, then, and do not let your-selves be burdened again by a yoke of slavery.**

Session Eleven
Galatians 5:16-26

Set Free to Live by the Spirit

SEARCH THE WORD

1 If you could live totally free for one day, how would your life be different?

Freedom isn't always what we picture it to be. Paul wanted the Galatians to live free, and he explained how they could do so in this section of Galatians.

Read verses 16-18.

2 What deliberate choice does God ask us to make in order to live free?

Choose to walk in the spirit

Why?

to experience His grace

3 What are some of the desires of the sinful nature?

greed
lust
power

4 How are the Spirit and the sinful nature, or flesh, in conflict with each other?

the flesh lusts against the Spirit - different objectives / purpose

opposing the Spirit of God

> **One reason that sin flourishes is that it is treated like a cream puff instead of a rattlesnake.**
> –biLLy sunday

5 What is the difference between living by the Spirit and living under the Law?

grace vs rules

pleasure us pleasing God

Read verses 19–21.

6 Paul identified some acts of our sinful natures. What areas of life does this list encompass?

our religion
human relationships

7 What are some specific examples of these sins?

8 How do you know this list isn't exhaustive?

**Fruit is more than words or deeds;
it includes the qualities of
character from which those words
and deeds issue.... Outstanding
among the "truly good qualities" of
Christian character are the nine
fruits of the Spirit. They include all
three, words, deeds and virtues. For
love, joy, peace and all the fruits of
the Spirit are revealed
in what we say, in what we do
and in what we are.**
—stephen f. winward

9 Why will those who habitually practice the desires of the sinful nature not inherit God's future Kingdom?

They aren't led by the spirit

Read verses 22-26.

10 In contrast, what characterizes people who let the Holy Spirit control their lives?

11 What is this spiritual fruit a sign of?

the indwelling of the H.S.

12 Identify at least one example for each aspect of the fruit of the Spirit.

*love
joy
peace
patience
kindness
goodness*

*faithfulness
gentleness
self control*

13 Why is there no law against this fruit?

I guess these are the things God desires for us

> **Spirit life is the product of both Spirit activity and human response. It comes from obedience to God's commands to love, be patient, kind, and self-controlled, but it also takes dependence on God's power, through the Spirit, to make it possible.**
>
> –stuart briscoe

14 Why is verse 24 a statement of fact?

15 What help do we have to live by the Spirit?

CONSIDER THE MESSAGE

Am I the only one who routinely gets things backward? I can't even tell you how many years of my Christian life were spent trying not to "gratify the desires of the sinful nature." Whether it was my desire to pitch a fit whenever life didn't go my way, my desperate desire for attention and love, my desire for junk food, or my desire to escape the heartaches of life through excessive sleep. Oh, how I fought against those raging desires but so often failed.

The Bible says, "live by the Spirit, and you will not gratify the desires of the sinful nature" (Galatians 5:16). Silly me. I thought it said, "Do not gratify the desires of the sinful nature, and you will live by the Spirit." God taught me how wrong I was about this concept through one of my favorite things: doughnuts. Chocolate-covered doughnuts, to be exact.

Late one night, I suddenly realized I had been tempted to eat a chocolate-covered doughnut since I woke up that morning. There was a time in my life when I wouldn't have been able to resist gratifying that "sinful" desire. Yet I had been able to do so that day. Why? Two reasons: I had enjoyed a ninety-minute workout earlier in the day and had been eating a healthy diet for several months. By focusing my energy on strengthening my body, resisting junk food was much easier.

I think this principle holds true in the spiritual realm as well. As we strengthen our spirits, we will automatically have more power to resist temptation. Most of us focus our efforts on resisting temptation. Then we are so exhausted by the effort and discouraged by our failures that we have no energy left to renew our spirits.

Taking positive action will yield far greater benefits than beating ourselves up for our failures. As an example, rather than berating yourself for being inconsistent with your quiet times, create a beautiful prayer room (or corner of a room). Make it such an inviting place that you want to be there more than anywhere else.

I decided years ago to make my prayer room the warmest, most welcoming place in my house. Although I'm no interior decorator, I think this particular room is flat-out gorgeous. It is brightly painted with lovely Victorian pictures on the wall. There's a little table covered in white lace with a flower arrangement, a mini-water fountain, and a candle on top. Next to my rocking chair, I keep a wicker basket containing my Bible, prayer journal, and several devotional books. The rest of my house is a perpetual wreck, but I always keep my prayer room in good order. It serves as a welcoming sanctuary in the midst of the chaos.

If you haven't done so already, I would encourage you to create the space and time necessary to feed your spirit. Read your Bible every day without fail, then carve out time for other uplifting Christian books. You can surround yourself with "a great cloud of witnesses" (Hebrews 12:1) by reading missionary biographies and classic devotionals.

As you spend time in your prayer place, your spirit will grow stronger, and you will notice your appetite for junk will gradually subside. Not disappear, mind you. Subside. The key is sticking with it: "The one who sows to please the Spirit, from the Spirit will reap eternal life. Let us not become weary in doing good, for at the proper time we will reap a harvest if we do not give up" (Galatians 6:8–9).

First you live by the Spirit; then you won't gratify the desires of the sinful nature. Let's put first things first.

APPLY THE TRUTH

1 How can you culti-
vate more of the fruit of
the Spirit in your life
this week?

> God does not drop neat, glittering, gift-wrapped packages of His sweet fruit into my life. We may pray for that to happen, and we may think it can. It never does. We are deluded if we think it will. When we ask God to give us the precious fruits of His own Spirit, these are bestowed always and only through the increased presence of His own person.
>
> –w. phiLLip keLLer

2 What desire of the sinful nature do you struggle with most?

How can you get victory over it this week?

> **Discipline is the human effort to create the space in which God can be generous and give you what you need.**
> –henri nouwen

3 Memorize Galatians 5:16 and 22–23:

So I say, live by the Spirit, and you will not gratify the desires of the sinful nature.

But the fruit of the Spirit is love, joy, peace, patience, kindness, goodness, faithfulness, gentleness and self-control.

Session Twelve
Galatians 6:1-18

Set Free to Reap a Harvest

SEARCH THE WORD

1 Describe a time when you didn't like living with the consequences of your actions.

Although we don't often think about the consequences of our choices—either negatively or positively—we have to live with them. Paul made this principle clear in the final chapter of Galatians, after writing about our mutual relationship with other believers.

Read verses 1-5.

2 How can we restore a fellow believer who is sinning?

3 How can we carry each other's burdens?

Many times others have "burdens" that are too big to bear. They do not have enough strength, resources, or knowledge to carry the load, and they need help. Denying ourselves to do for others what they *cannot* do for themselves is showing the sacrificial love of Christ. On the other hand, everyone has responsibilities that only he or she can carry. These things are our own particular "load" that we need to take daily responsibility for and work out.

The Greek words for *burden* and *load* give us insight into the meaning of these texts. The Greek word for *burden* means ... boulders. We [all] need help with the boulders—those times of crisis and tragedy in our lives. In contrast, the Greek word for load means "cargo." These loads are like knapsacks. Problems arise when people act as if their "boulders" are daily loads, and refuse help, or as if their "daily loads" are boulders they shouldn't have to carry.

–henry cLoud & john townsend

4 In what ways do we think we're something when we're nothing?

5 How can you reconcile Paul's statements to "carry each other's burdens" and "each one should carry his own load"?

Read verses 6-10.

6 When someone teaches God's Word, how should we respond? Why?

7 Explain the principle of sowing and reaping in your own words.

8 How does Paul encourage those who can't see the results of their labor?

> **The harvest will not be according to how much we know, but how much we sow. We may have a large supply of seed in the barn of the mind, but unless it is planted in suitable soil it will bear no harvest. Sow the seed of thoughts in word and deeds.**
>
> –henrietta mears

Read verses 11–16.

9 Why were some believers pressuring the Galatians to be circumcised?

10 What are some contemporary examples of trying to compel believers to be circumcised?

11 When is it okay to boast?

12 What did Paul say was the bottom line in the circumcision debate?

> Your worst days are never so bad that you are beyond the reach of God's grace. And your best days are never so good that you are beyond the need of God's grace.
> –jerry bridges

Read verses 17-18.

13 As Paul concluded this letter, why did he draw attention to the brandmarks on his body? (See 2 Corinthians 11:23–29 to identify some of those marks.)

14 Describe the grace Paul prayed for the Galatians to have.

CONSIDER THE MESSAGE

As I've reread the previous eleven "Consider the Message" segments, carefully praying about what to leave you with, I decided it was important to emphasize this fact: I am not advocating license; I am advocating freedom from the law.

Since the church pendulum continually swings back and forth between those two extremes, people are often unclear where the middle ground is. While some churches remain steeped in law, others have overreacted to dry dogma and dead ritual to the extent that the average American Christian is literally indistinguishable from his pagan counterpart. My friends, this should not be so. "Shall we go on sinning so that grace may increase? By no means! We died to sin; how can we live in it any longer?" (Romans 6:1–2).

There is a third option: freedom *in Christ*. Not freedom *from* Christ or even freedom *thanks to* Christ. True Christian liberty is found only as we remain in close communion with Christ, as we abide in Him and He abides in us (John 15).

God's Word tells us that it requires great care to live in freedom. Indeed, we see a pattern throughout the Bible. Obedience and freedom are linked, just as disobedience and slavery are linked. When the people of Israel obeyed God, they lived in peace; when they rebelled against Him, they were invariably taken into captivity. Study the prophets and see how God warns His people again and again: *I want you to remain free; therefore, live holy lives. If you live sin-filled lives, you'll eventually end up in chains—enslaved to that sin or to anyone who wishes to take you captive.*

God loves us, but that doesn't mean we can jump off a thirty-story building and expect Him to suspend the laws of the universe. He won't. We're going to crash. The same is true in the spiritual realm. God will not suspend the laws of the spiritual universe on our behalf. We reap what we sow, forgiveness notwithstanding.

God's love is unconditional, but His blessings are not. Throughout Scripture, God clearly states we get to choose between blessings and curses. God tells us exactly what we need to do and how we need to live if we want to enjoy His best for our lives. He will love us whether or not we choose wisely, but He will not alter the logical consequences of our choices.

If we want to reap loving relationships, we must sow love. If we want to reap spiritual power, we must sow prayer. If we want to reap peace, we must sow trust. If we want to reap spiritual growth, we must sow spiritual disciplines. If we want to reap emotional healing, we must sow forgiveness and repentance. If we want to reap victory over sin, we must sow accountability and actively fight temptations. If we want to reap the abundant life Jesus promised, we must sow obedience.

God wants you to reap a bountiful harvest of blessings, but it's up to you which seeds you sow in the soil of your heart. Don't ever forget: God will love you unconditionally no matter what seeds you plant. So don't sow out of obligation or duty; sow joyfully with your eyes fixed on the eternal harvest awaiting you.

APPLY THE TRUTH

1 What do you want to reap spiritually in your life?

2 What can you do this week to sow good seed for those crops in your life?

3 Memorize Galatians 6:7–9:

> **Do not be deceived: God cannot be mocked. A man reaps what he sows. The one who sows to please his sinful nature, from that nature will reap destruction; the one who sows to please the Spirit, from the Spirit will reap eternal life. Let us not become weary in doing good, for at the proper time we will reap a harvest if we do not give up.**

Leader's Guide

TO ENCOURAGE GROUP DISCUSSION

- If your group isn't used to discussing together, explain at the beginning of the first session that these studies are designed for discussion, not lecture. Encourage each member to participate, but keep in mind that it may take several meetings before shy members feel comfortable enough to participate.
- Encourage discussion by asking several people to contribute answers to a question. "What do the rest of you think?" or "Is there anything else that could be added?" are two ways of doing this.
- Receive all contributions warmly. Never bluntly reject what anyone says, even if you think the answer is incorrect. Instead, ask what others think and/or ask the person to identify the verse(s) that led her to that conclusion.
- Be sure you don't talk too much as the leader. Redirect questions that you are asked. A discussion should move in the form of a bouncing ball, back and forth between members, not in the form of a fan with the discussion always coming back to the leader at that point. The leader acts as a moderator. As members of a group get to know one another better, the discussion will move more freely.
- Don't be afraid of pauses or long silences. People need time to think about the questions. Never answer your own question—either rephrase it or move on to another area for discussion.
- Watch hesitant members for an indication by facial expression or body language that they have something to say, and

then give them an encouraging nod or speak their names.

- Discourage too-talkative members from monopolizing the discussion by specifically directing questions to others. If necessary, speak to them privately about the need for discussion and enlist their help in encouraging everyone to participate.

- End the sessions by praying for one another, thanking God for growth, and asking Him for help to practice the truth discovered during the week. Vary the prayer times by staying together, breaking into smaller groups or pairs, using sentence prayers, etc. Resist the ever-present temptation to spend more time talking about prayer than actually praying. When it's time to pray, don't waste time on elaborate prayer requests for Susie's uncle's cousin's neighbor's grandmother. Instead, allow the Holy Spirit to bring forth what is on His heart as He prompts individual members to pray.

DISCUSSION LEADER'S NOTES

1. Set Free by Good News: Galatians 1:1-10

Purpose: To understand that salvation is through faith in Jesus plus nothing.

Question 1: Each study begins with an icebreaker question such as this one. Ask a few volunteers to share their answers. As your group members get to know one another better, you may want to go around the circle and have everyone respond to this opening question. Pray for sensitivity in how you use it so you don't embarrass anyone or put people on the spot.

Question 2: Before asking this question, review the background information on this letter in the introduction to this guide. You may want to do additional background reading in a commentary or two.

Question 10: Ask a volunteer to read 2 John 7–11, and briefly discuss how John's instructions about those who pervert the gospel expand on what Paul wrote.

Question 11: For a full description of the gospel Paul preached, read 1 Corinthians 15:1–7.

Question 12: Whom we please and serve is a theme throughout Scripture. See, for example, Joshua 24:14–15; Matthew 6:24; and Ephesians 6:5–7. If you have time, ask volunteers to read these passages aloud.

Conclusion: Sing together "There Is a Redeemer," "Lamb of God," or another song about salvation. (Many studies conclude with a song to sing together. If your group doesn't know the suggested song(s), choose another one on the same theme.)

2. Set Free by God's Call: Galatians 1:11–24

Purpose: To recognize that God calls each of us to serve Him and build His Kingdom, just as He called Paul for a particular ministry. (Note: Allow women to debate the issue of whether or not God simply chooses those He knows will choose Him, but don't allow it to deteriorate into an argument. Sincere Christians disagree on this. Read Romans 9–11 to prepare.)

Question 3: Paul's Jewish credentials were impeccable. For more details, see Acts 22:3; 26:5; and Philippians 3:4–6. For a description of his actions toward believers before he became one, see Acts 7:58–8:3. You may want to take the time to have volunteers read these passages aloud.

Question 4: For Paul's testimony about God's call to salvation, see Acts 9:1–19; 22:3–21; and 26:1–23.

Question 5: Paul was not the only person God set apart for His work even before he was born. For example, He chose Jeremiah (Jeremiah 1:5), a psalmist (Psalm 71:6), and Jesus the Messiah (Isaiah 49:1).

Conclusion: Sing together "We Are an Offering."

3. Set Free to Proclaim the Gospel: Galatians 2:1–10

Purpose: To understand that God called us to proclaim the Gospel within our spheres of influence.

Question 2: Bible scholars do not agree on when Paul made this second visit to Jerusalem or the starting point for counting fourteen years later. Some believe he was recounting the events of Acts 11; others, Acts 15. The time, however, is incidental to the point Paul made in these verses: He did not go to get the approval of the other apostles for the ministry to which God had called him.

Barnabas started out as Paul's mentor (Acts 9:27) but became his ministry partner in Antioch (Acts 11:25–26) and fellow missionary (Acts 12:25). Titus was a Gentile believer whom Paul introduced to the Lord (Titus 1:4).

Question 3: Many of the Jewish believers in Paul's day believed that Gentiles could be saved but were second-class citizens in God's Kingdom unless they were circumcised. Paul refuted this long-standing concept.

Question 12: Notice the logical progression from doctrine to practice, one of the main movements in many of Paul's letters.

Conclusion: If you have a soloist in your group, ask her to sing "People Need the Lord." Or play a recording of this song. Close in prayer for unsaved friends and family members.

4. Set Free by Grace Alone: Galatians 2:11-21

Purpose: To understand that we are justified by faith and live our lives to please God by faith.

Question 2: Read Acts 11:19–30 and 13:1–3 for background on the church in Antioch.

Question 7: Be sure your group members understand that even though we obtain right standing before God by faith (justification), that position does not give us a license to live sinfully.

Question 9: For a more complete understanding of this passage, read Romans 7:7–14.

Question 10: The verb "crucified" in Greek is in the perfect tense, meaning it was a past action that continues to have an effect.

Question 12: Following the group's discussion of this question, you may want to summarize with the following quote: "Above all, it is God's grace that makes it possible for sinners to be justified. It is unthinkable for anyone to set aside what God has already provided and to return to the old ways. Doing so would devalue the cross as the center of our hope (6:14). No wonder in the following statement (3:1), Paul began with an outburst, 'you foolish Galatians!'"[1]

Conclusion: Sing together "Amazing Grace."

5. Set Free From the Requirements of the Law: Galatians 3:1–14

Purpose: To understand that we can't grow spiritually in our own efforts apart from the working of the Holy Spirit.

Question 2: When Paul called the Galatians foolish, he meant spiritually dull. Bewitched means to be put under a spell, to be cursed.

Question 5: For more background on Abraham's faith, ask a volunteer to read Romans 4:9–12.

Question 8: Use this quote to summarize: "Law demands obedience, and this means obedience in *all things*. The law is not a 'religious cafeteria' where people can pick and choose (see James 2:10–11)."[2]

Question 9: "The Judaizers wanted to seduce the Galatians into a religion of legal works, while Paul wanted them to enjoy a relationship of love and life by faith in Christ. For the Christian to abandon faith and grace for law and works is to lose everything exciting that the Christian can experience in his daily fellowship with the Lord."[3]

Conclusion: Ask two volunteers to read 1 Corinthians 1:26–31 and 2 Corinthians 3:17–18 before closing with prayer.

6. Set Free to Enjoy an Inheritance: Galatians 3:15-25

Purpose: To be grateful for the inheritance God has given us.

Question 3: The Greek word translated "covenant" also means "testament" or "will." It was a legal document that was sealed, so no one could change it. Paul used the word in the Old Testament sense of God's covenant with His people, but he also included legal nuances of a will. Just as a will could not be changed, added to, or deleted by another person, the Law did not invalidate God's covenant promises to Abraham.

Question 6: Ask a volunteer to read Romans 3:19–20.

Question 8: A mediator is a go-between to help two parties agree. Instead of giving the Law directly to His people, God gave it to them through angels (Acts 7:53) and Moses. This act made it inferior to the promise God gave directly to Abraham.

Question 10: The phrase "put in charge" in verse 24 means in the sense of a guardian or tutor. In Greek and Roman families, a slave was assigned this role to walk his master's children to and from school, keep them out of trouble, discipline them, and generally be in charge of them until they came of age, around age thirteen or fourteen.

Conclusion: Play the song "Generations," by Sara Groves.

7. Set Free to Live As Children of God: Galatians 3:26-4:7

Purpose: To thank God for the benefits He gives us when we become part of His family.

Question 2: Don't let the group argue about the phrase "baptized into Christ" in verse 27. For an explanation, see 1 Corinthians 12:12–13.

The phrase "clothed yourselves with Christ" in verse 27 refers to the special toga a male child received when he came of age. Each father set that time for his son, but it was normally around the age of fourteen. That garment was a symbol of adulthood, being recognized as a son and heir with full family and state rights and privileges. As believers, God treats us as adults when we put on the "toga" of Christ's righteousness.

Question 6: According to Roman law, minor children were required to have legal guardians and had the same status as slaves until they came of age. Then they could enjoy the rights and privileges of sons and inherit their fathers' property.

Question 11: *Abba* is the Aramaic word for *Papa*, a name of intimacy children of any age, including adults, called their fathers and students sometimes called their teachers. It was not used in Judaism as a name for God.

Conclusion: Read together Psalm 103. Then close with sentence prayers of thanks for what God has given us. You might want to go through the alphabet to name benefits we enjoy because of our relationship with God.

8. Set Free Never to Be Enslaved Again: Galatians 4:8-20

Purpose: To resist the temptation to go back to enslaving habits and rules and enjoy God's freedom in Christ.

Question 2: Read verse 8 in THE MESSAGE and/or the NEW LIVING TRANSLATION for clarity.

Question 6: Keep this discussion general instead of identifying specific people, groups, or churches that are legalistic. Don't let it degenerate into an argument.

Question 8: It's not necessarily wrong to observe special days. The issue is whether or not we do so to earn points with God.

Question 9: When Paul said he "became like you," he was treating the Galatians as equals, not as their mentor or teacher. Although we don't know what Paul's illness was, some Bible scholars think it was an eye disease, based on his comments in 6:11.

Conclusion: Ask a couple of group members to read Romans 6, alternating paragraphs (verses 1–4, 5–7, 8–10, 11–14, 15–18, 19–23). Or in advance, ask someone in your group to prepare this chapter as a choral reading and bring copies to the session.

9. Set Free by a Promise: Galatians 4:21-31

Purpose: To recognize that God's promises to Abraham and Sarah resulted in the freedom He offers us in Christ.

Question 3: The son's status was based on his mother's status, so a son of a slave woman could never enjoy the rights and privileges a son of a free woman had.

Question 4: Read Genesis 16 and 21 for background on these two sons.

Question 12: The quote in verse 30 is Sarah's words to Abraham in Genesis 21:10. Paul used it to urge the Galatians to expel the Judaizers, Paul's opponents, from the church.

Conclusion: Read together Psalm 145.

10. Set Free to Love Others: Galatians 5:1-15

Purpose: To learn to balance our freedom in Christ with love for others.

Question 2: In Judaism, circumcision and keeping the Law went hand in hand and were integral to the Jewish religion. People couldn't choose one without the other.

Expect questions on verse 4. The following explanation will help you to explain it:

Paul had shown that the Law was a pedagogue [teacher]. Once, Law was the avenue through which a believer experienced his relationship with God. But now that relationship is direct and personal, as with a child who at last receives the "full rights" of sonship (4:5). What, then, if a son keeps going back to his old pedagogue for directions? Clearly, he has alienated himself from the personal relationship. Such a fall from grace back into old practices and ways means simply that the individual *is no better off than he was before!* All the freedom, all the joy, all the adventure of the life a child of God is to live by faith, has been drained away—traded for something that is worse than nothing. "Christ will be of no value to you at all" means simply that being a Christian will not make the *difference* in daily life He intends it to. A person will be no better off than he was before being a Christian, as far as living the Christian life is concerned.

This seems a hard thing to say. No better off? Why, heaven has been won, at least.

Yes, but the Christian faith is not solely concerned with eternity. The Christian faith includes God's affirmation that life now is important too—important to God, important to others, and important to you.[4]

Question 10: Yeast was a symbol of evil and sin. See Luke 12:1 and 1 Corinthians 5:8.

Question 12: In verse 11, the Greek word for offense literally means "the arm or stick on which bait was fixed in a trap."[5] It also means a stumbling block.

Question 13: The Greek words for "biting" and "devouring" refer to wild animals fighting one another.

Conclusion: To help your group members focus on how they are to love others because Christ has freed them from slavery to the Law, read together 1 Corinthians 13.

11. Set Free to Live by the Spirit: Galatians 5:16-26

Purpose: To grow more fruit of the Spirit and gain victory over the desires of the sinful nature.

Question 2: To "live by the Spirit" means to keep on walking in the Spirit's control. It's not a one-time or static action but an ongoing one.

Question 4: We can't get victory over our sinful natures by an act of the will, in our own strength. Therefore, we need to surrender to the Spirit's leading, or control.

Question 9: Be sure group members understand that we cannot lose our salvation by sinning. People who claim to be Christians but who continually live in sin show by their lifestyles that they are not God's children. The phrase "live like this" in verse 21 means to practice as a habit, to do repeatedly.

Question 10: Notice that verse 22 says "fruit," not "fruits."

The character qualities Paul listed here are all related offshoots of love, which begins the list. Notice that spiritual fruit involves character, in contrast to acts of the sinful nature. The Judaizers focused on external behavior for pleasing God, while God focuses on heart attitude and character.

Conclusion: Ask a couple of volunteers to read Romans 8:1–17 aloud before the group prays together.

12. Set Free to Reap a Harvest: Galatians 6:1–18

Purpose: To live in such a way as to reap spiritual growth instead of sin.

Question 2: The Greek word for *restore* is used of mending nets, setting broken bones, and bringing groups together. You might want to spend a couple of minutes discussing the biblical way to confront Christians who are sinning. See also Matthew 18:15–17; 1 Timothy 5:19–20; and 2 Samuel 12:1–14.

Question 5: The Greek word for *burdens* in verse 2 means a heavy, crushing load, a weight of temptation. The Greek word for *load* was used for a soldier's pack that he had to carry himself. While we are to help one another with overwhelming burdens, we still have personal responsibilities that no one else can do for us.

Question 6: Providing financially for Bible teachers was a new concept. Jewish people were taxed to support their priests, and Gentiles paid fees to support their religious leaders.

Question 12: See 2 Corinthians 5:17–21 for a fuller explanation of a "new creation."

Conclusion: Sing together "Change My Heart, O God."

Endnotes

Session Twelve

1. Henry Cloud and John Townsend, *Boundaries* (Grand Rapids, Mich.: Zondervan, 1992), 30–31.

Leader's Guide

1. *Zondervan Illustrated Bible Backgrounds Commentary*, vol. 3, ed. Clinton E. Arnold (Grand Rapids: Zondervan, 2002), 280.
2. Warren W. Wiersbe, *Be Free* (Wheaton, Ill.: Victor Books, 1975) 70.
3. Ibid., 71.
4. Lawrence O. Richards, *The Teacher's Commentary* (Wheaton, Ill.: Victor Books, 1987), 905.
5. *Zondervan Illustrated Bible Backgrounds Commentary*, 290.

Bibliography

Life Application Commentary: Galatians, Wheaton, Ill.: Tyndale House, 1994.

MacArthur, John. *Galatians (The MacArthur New Testament Commentary),* Chicago: Moody, 1987.

McKnight, Scot. *Galatians (The NIV Application Commentary),* Grand Rapids, Mich.: Zondervan, 1995.

Wiersbe, Warren W. *Be Free,* Colorado Springs: Victor, 1975.

4. Set Free by Grace Alone

Galatians 2:20–21

I have been crucified with Christ and I no longer live, but Christ lives in me. The life I live in the body, I live by faith in the Son of God, who loved me and gave himself for me. I do not set aside the grace of God, for if righteousness could be gained through the law, Christ died for nothing!

Extracting the Precious From Galatians, Donna Partow

1. Set Free by Good News

Galatians 1:8

But even if we or an angel from heaven should preach a gospel other than the one we preached to you, let him be eternally condemned!

Extracting the Precious From Galatians, Donna Partow

5. Set Free From the Requirements of the Law

Galatians 3:14

He redeemed us in order that the blessing given to Abraham might come to the Gentiles through Christ Jesus, so that by faith we might receive the promise of the Spirit.

Extracting the Precious From Galatians, Donna Partow

2. Set Free by God's Call

Galatians 1:15–16

But when God, who set me apart from birth and called me by his grace, was pleased to reveal his Son in me so that I might preach him among the Gentiles, I did not consult any man.

Extracting the Precious From Galatians, Donna Partow

6. Set Free to Enjoy an Inheritance

Galatians 3:18

For if the inheritance depends on the law, then it no longer depends on a promise; but God in his grace gave it to Abraham through a promise.

Extracting the Precious From Galatians, Donna Partow

3. Set Free to Proclaim the Gospel

Galatians 2:5

We did not give in to them [false teachers] for a moment, so that the truth of the gospel might remain with you.

Extracting the Precious From Galatians, Donna Partow

12. Set Free to Reap a Harvest Galatians 6:7–9 Do not be deceived: God cannot be mocked. A man reaps what he sows. The one who sows to please his sinful nature, from that nature will reap his destruction; the one who sows to please the Spirit, from the Spirit will reap eternal life. Let us not become weary in doing good, for at the proper time we will reap a harvest if we do not give up. *Extracting the Precious From Galatians, Donna Partow*	**11. Set Free to Live by the Spirit** Galatians 5:16, 22–23 So I say, live by the Spirit, and you will not gratify the desires of the sinful nature. . . . But the fruit of the Spirit is love, joy, peace, patience, kindness, goodness, faithfulness, gentleness and self-control. *Extracting the Precious From Galatians, Donna Partow*	**10. Set Free to Love Others** Galatians 5:1 It is for freedom that Christ has set us free. Stand firm, then, and do not let yourselves be burdened again by a yoke of slavery. *Extracting the Precious From Galatians, Donna Partow*
9. Set Free by a Promise Galatians 4:31 Therefore, brothers, we are not children of the slave woman, but of the free woman. *Extracting the Precious From Galatians, Donna Partow*	**8. Set Free Never to Be Enslaved Again** Galatians 4:9 But now that you know God—or rather are known by God—how is it that you are turning back to those weak and miserable principles? Do you wish to be enslaved by them all over again? *Extracting the Precious From Galatians, Donna Partow*	**7. Set Free to Live As Children of God** Galatians 4:1, 7 What I am saying is that as long as the heir is a child, he is no different from a slave, although he owns the whole estate. . . . So you are no longer a slave, but a son; and since you are a son, God has made you also an heir. *Extracting the Precious From Galatians, Donna Partow*

These Bible Studies Just Keep Changing Lives

Following God...Regardless

In Partow's newest devotional, she uses her trademark transparency to illustrate how readers should follow God, no matter how difficult life becomes. She understands the temptation to take the easy life, but shows how enriched we will be by *Standing Firm*.

Standing Firm

It's Time to Break Free

According to Partow, anything that holds you back from doing all God has created you to do is "slavery." This study explores the most common bondage found in women's lives and explores ways others, with God's help, have escaped.

Living in Absolute Freedom

Develop an Unshakable Trust in the God Who Loves You

Your self-confidence is fragile and inconsistent. God-confidence is the reliance on the steady, unchanging grace of God and learning to rely on His discretion in your life.

Walking in Total God-Confidence

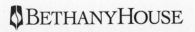

7/12 Linda's Daley (Kristara's S.I.L.)
· Chloe making progress
· election
- Keri - had jaw surgery this summ.
              braces off soon
- Kate - buy a new house?
              Steve's job still a question
-
- Sue - both son's wandered from truth
              Jeremy + Chad
————————————————————————

9/26 - safe trip for Andrea's parents
     - Hausler's friends traveling
     - Vince in Haiti
     - Diane's brother re-married -
              wife miscarried (John + Deb
     - Eric's Dad - hosp w/ heart trouble
  [scribble]   would recog. he has
        Bill   limitations

     - Donna is itching

nephew - Gladys: SIL's son - homo
                   meds liver transplan
          Joe Romeo

     -

9/30
- Haiti
- Kirsten) Debate
    Ehlers ~~voted~~ no
        ~~to vote~~
    ~~●●●~~ on Marriage amend
- Eric's father rec. fm
    minor heart attack
- See Parker's sons
-

10-28-

- Haiti
- Election
- Baby

11/004
- Peter fell off roof
- Haiti team back
- Sarah's baby
- Melanie ~ prof of faith / single
    w/ Proms
- Mom to meet ext family

11/18 - Sue Packer Out of town
- Andra - Reese burned hand
Emma fever
- Dad
- Herbert sick
- Eric O. of town Florida

16th brunch - Sue's house
Mary — Exchange $5
a bake

David Moody - seriously ill
Kristi - new baby
Kim - R shoulder
tendonitis

brunch !!

Chad + Danielle (son Isaac)

Sue
Packer